AME AD

My Reading Tree!

D0065356

In memory of my dad ~ M C

For Lynn and Oberon ~ D R

LITTLE TIGER PRESS
An imprint of Magi Publications
1 The Coda Centre, 189 Munster Road, London SW6 6AW
www.littletigerpress.com

This edition published 2008
First published in Great Britain 2004
Text copyright © Michael Catchpool 2004
Illustrations copyright © David Roberts 2004
Michael Catchpool and David Roberts have asserted their rights
to be identified as the author and illustrator of this work under the
Copyright, Designs and Patents Act, 1988.
A CIP catalogue record for this book is available from the British Library.

Printed in China • All rights reserved
ISBN 978-1-84506-667-3

2 4 6 8 10 9 7 5 3 1

Hopping Mad!

Michael Catchpool

illustrated by David Roberts

LITTLE TIGER PRESS
London

Fred lived next door to Finn.
Fred had five frogs and so did Finn.

One night when the moon was up and the grass was damp, Finn's five frogs called to Fred's frogs, "Come on over, we're having a party!"

"What an excellent idea!" Fred's frogs croaked back. "We'll be right over!" And they hopped over the fence.

The frogs dived and splashed and flipped
and flopped and had a fantastic time.
By the time the sun was coming up
they could hardly manage a hop.

"Phew!" croaked Fred's frogs.
"We really must be getting
home," and they dragged
themselves back over
the fence.

The next morning, as the sun sparkled on the water, Fred stood idly counting his frogs.

"One, two, three, FOUR!"

Then he looked over the fence
and counted the frogs in Finn's pond.
"One, two, three, four, five, SIX!"
Fred was furious.

"Frog thief!" he shouted at Finn. "You should have five frogs and you've got six. You've stolen one of mine!" And Fred marched into Finn's garden and snatched a frog before Finn could say a word.

"I'll soon put an end to your stealing!" shouted Fred, and with some wood and some nails he built his fence higher and higher.

That evening, as an owl swooped across the sky, Fred's five frogs called to Finn's five frogs, "Come over to our pond tonight for some fun."

"What an excellent idea!" croaked Finn's frogs.

The frogs frolicked and
feasted on flies until they
were completely exhausted.
"Time to be getting home,"
they croaked.
Then Finn's frogs squeezed
back under the fence.

The next day, as the birds were singing in the trees, Finn slowly counted his frogs, "One, two, THREE!"

He glared over the fence into Fred's pond. "One, two, three, four, five, six, SEVEN!"

Finn was fuming. "Frog thief!" he shouted at Fred. "You have seven frogs and I've only got three."

He marched right round to Fred's garden and snatched back his two frogs.

"I'll stop you pinching my frogs!" said Finn, and he dug a big, wide ditch by the fence.

That evening, Finn's five frogs called to Fred's, "Why not party in our pond tonight?"

So Fred's frogs scrambled over the huge fence and leaped over the enormous ditch.

The frogs had a splendid time, diving
and swimming, dancing and singing
until they could hardly croak.

Just before dawn, Fred's frogs
returned home. They leaped
back over the enormous
ditch and scrambled back
over the huge fence.

The following morning,
while the dew glistened on
the grass, Fred carefully
counted his frogs.
"One, TWO!"

Then he counted the
frogs in Finn's pond.
  "One, two, three, four,
five, six, seven, EIGHT!"
  Fred was frantic.

"Frog thief!" he shouted at Finn. "You've stolen three of my frogs," and he marched through the gate and snatched back his frogs. "I'll put a stop to this," Fred said, and he put a great big cage right over his frogs and his pond.

That evening, Fred's five frogs called to
Finn's frogs. "We can't play tonight, we've
been locked up."

"Then we'll come over to you," croaked
Finn's frogs, and they leaped across the great
big ditch, over the high fence and opened the
door of the cage.

"Phew!" said Fred's frogs. "You know,
us frogs need our freedom," and off they
hopped, with Finn's frogs close behind.

Now Fred has no frogs.
And neither does Finn.

But Fiona, who lives four doors down, has TEN!

Croak! Croak! Croak!

Super Search!

Look at the picture below. Put the word stickers next to the correct objects in the picture. We've done one for you.

★ When you have put all the words in the right places, add the first star to your reading tree!

 # Picture Dictionary

Look at the words below. They are all types of insects!
Put the correct picture stickers next to each word.

beetle   dragonfly

moth   bee

★ Have you got these right? Then put a star on your reading tree!

Sentence Order

All stories are made up of **sentences**. Tick the sentence
below that came **last** in the story.

☐	But Fiona, who lives four doors down, has TEN!
☐	Now Fred has no frogs.
☐	And neither does Finn.

★ Did you get this right?
Remember to add another star to your reading tree!

True or False

Fred tried different things to stop Finn stealing his frogs.
Which of these sentences is true and which is false?

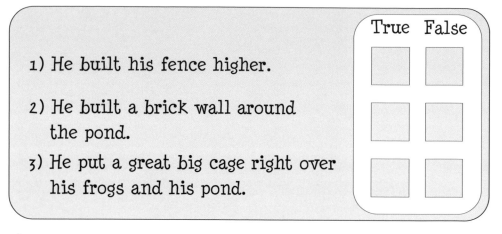

True   False

1) He built his fence higher.

2) He built a brick wall around
   the pond.

3) He put a great big cage right over
   his frogs and his pond.

★ Did you get this right? Add another star to your reading tree.

Crazy Commas

A **comma** is a mark that is used to separate words. A comma
sometimes tells the reader where to pause in a sentence.

E.g. When the moon was up and the grass was damp, Finn's
five frogs called to Fred's frogs.

Put a comma into each sentence below.

1) Come on over we're having a party!
2) Just before dawn Fred's frogs returned home.
3) We can't play tonight we've been locked up.

★ Did you find where the pauses should be?
Then add another star to your reading tree!

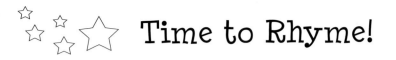

Time to Rhyme!

Words that have the same sounds as one another are called **rhyming words**. E.g. back – tack. The words below all rhyme with words from the story! Put the word stickers next to the word it rhymes with.

1) dig _____

2) floor _____

3) dog _____

4) fowl _____

5) date _____

6) sun _____

★ Did you get these right?
Remember to add a star to your reading tree.

Perfect Plurals

A **noun** is a naming word — a person, place or thing.
A **plural noun** shows there is more than one person, place or thing. An **s** at the end of a noun often means that it is plural.

E.g. one cat — two cats

Circle the plural nouns in the sentences below.

1) Fred used some nails.

2) You have seven frogs and I've only got three.

3) Fiona lives four doors down.

4) The birds were singing in the trees.

Did you find these plural nouns in the story?

★ Did you get these right?
Then add the last star to your reading tree!